MW00388453

SINGLE, SATISFIED & SET APART

VINOKIA M. JOHNSON

Copyright © 2019 Vinokia Johnson All rights reserved.

DEDICATION

In memory of my grandmother Malinda Washington who has gone to be with the Lord. Thank you for living a Godly life before your family. You left fingerprints of God's grace on our lives. You fully exemplified the role of a woman who is Single, Satisfied, and Set Apart. The prayers you've prayed are yet shielding us and you shall never be forgotten.

CONTENTS

INTRODUCTION

Married and separated at nine months pregnant-I was so devastated I thought I was going to lose my mind. Feelings of betrayal, abandonment, and defeat left me with shame and despair. I was disappointed, hopeless, and emotionally drained. Days of doom and gloom eventually drove me to having a mental breakdown. Filled with so much of bitter and hatred, no one could help me but God!! As I faithfully attended church, the word of God began to transform and renew my mind. I learned how-to walk-in forgiveness, and as I applied the principles of God to my life, my life began to turn around.

This book is not for everyone, but it's for the woman who's been kicked down but not destroyed. The woman who wants to understand her value and self-worth. The woman who feels hopeless and longs to be loved. The woman who is struggling to make ends meet. The wounded woman who's struggling with forgiving others and herself. The woman who wants to maximize her single life as she waits for her spouse. And the woman who understands that no matter what she has gone through, there is still light at the end of the tunnel.

As you read this book may it empower, enlighten, and inspire you to become a better you. May you overcome everything the enemy has thrown your way to stop you from fulfilling your destiny. As your life began to transform, may God take you higher in every area of your life. And as God heal you, may you heal others.

1 UNDERSTANDING YOUR VALUE AND

SELF-WORTH

We live in a society where dressing modestly, being virtuous, and doing the right thing is considered to be oldfashioned. A world where wrong is considered right and right is considered wrong. Where twerking and dropping it like it's hot has become the norm because the value of a woman has diminished tremendously. The powerful influences of satan "seems" to be the right way for her to go but it's only to her demise.

Proverbs 14:12 says "There's a way that seemeth right unto a man, but the end thereof is the way of death."

When a woman doesn't know her self-worth, she will conform to what is not right and find herself in compromising situations that are detrimental to her life. There is a constant battle between what is wrong and what is right. The world has a saying that females are made up of sugar, spice, and everything nice as long as they're acting kind and pleasant, but God says we were created in His image and in His likeness regardless of how we act. God calls us worthy, valuable, loving, and beautiful, but the enemy says just the opposite. And yes, at times we struggle with who God says we are because we are sinful, vulnerable, delicate, and shameful but we are made in God's image!! We are quick to believe what the *world* says about us than what the *word* says about us as righteous women. The enemy doesn't want you to see God's image in you, he wants you to see the image of a woman who is flawed, failing, inflicted, and defeated. The enemy's desire is for women to be foolish, loud, naïve, simple, with low self-esteem and not fulfill her destiny. God's desire is for women to have high moral standards to know that she is the apple of His eye and to fulfill her God's given purpose. And because many of us don't see ourselves as God sees us, the enemy has caused chaos in our lives. The enemy doesn't want you to value yourselves and to become the Proverbs 31 woman that the Bible speaks of.

John 10:10-says "The thief cometh not, but for to steal, and to kill, and to destroy: I am come that they might have life, and that they might have it more abundantly."

God's desire is for you to experience the fullness of His love so that it may impact others. The influence of a "Godly Woman" who is called to holiness and righteousness- is like no other. She's a virtuous woman, a woman with honesty, discipline, and moral excellence. God's desire is for all women to be virtuous and being single doesn't exempt you from being or becoming a virtuous woman. The word of God says who can find a virtuous woman? A virtuous woman is unique, wise, productive, and creative. She's a builder, she builds her home whether she's married or not. *Proverbs 14:1 says- "Every wise woman buildeth her house: but the foolish plucketh it down with her hands."*

A woman who values her self-worth is not exempted from making mistakes; she's not perfect, she's Godly. She respects herself and others. The enemy wants her to doubt she's good, and doubt that she is valuable, but she is worthy of everything that God has for her. It was never the enemy's intent for a woman to love and to respect herself. When a woman loves and respects herself, she will never degrade herself or humiliate herself for attention. She carries herself like a queen and she will allow the enemy to bring disgrace to herself or to her family. More and more women are convinced that if they are not showing their butt cheeks and cleavage, they're not attractive and men will ignore them. But dressing like that will only attract the wrong kind of man, a man who will take advantage of her, use and abuse her because he thinks that she's easy and vulnerable. A Godly woman who respects herself knows that dressing modestly and respectably will draw the right kind of attention to her and that her elegance will never go unnoticed. She won't disrespect herself neither will she allow disrespect from others. The way you present yourself and how you dress says a lot about you. You must carry yourself with dignity, integrity, and pride!! You don't have to expose yourself to get attention. You are a queen with moral compasses and values!! A queen refuses to sacrifice her standards to fit in. She understands that even though she has faced many obstacles, there is a level of respect that she has for herself that she clings to because she's special.

Women standards are also decreasing more and more partly due to the fact that we live in a day and age where the older women are not teaching the younger women how to live a *"Godly Life."* Many older women are not setting a good example for the younger women, they are encouraging them to be wild and loose. The bible says that the older women are to *"teach the younger women."* Instead, they are being taught to seek after *a man* and not seek after *The Man.* And because many women lack Godly instructions, they will never reach their full potential because they don't know who they are. I have heard many older women say, *"Having a piece of man is better than having no man at all!"* What?!!! And we wonder why the generations that are coming along are in a hopeless situation!! So many men are so used to dealing with women who have no standards that when they meet a woman who does they're intimidated and refuse to make the necessary adjustments. Women of God, don't lower your standards nor settle for less than what you are believing your Heavenly Father for.

Real men are never intimidated about how high your standards are even if they have to make adjustments. As a matter of fact, a real man loves a woman who won't settle, a woman who loves herself, someone who is different than what has been presented to him. Men, whether they are good or bad, he knows what a woman's standard should be like. Many of them settle with a foolish woman not so much that he loves her but because she doesn't require anything from him. He knows that what she's doing for him he supposed to be doing for her. God has placed certain things on the inside of men and that is to be a protector and to be a provider- whether he accepts it or not he knows his role.

"Woman of God, no matter how scarce men are, there are still men who know who they are and will appreciate the queen that you are."

I was at the beauty salon one Saturday evening, and I couldn't believe what I was hearing. There were a couple of single ladies who were there and all they talked about was men!!! What men like, what men don't like, what a man will do and what he won't do. They were convinced that a good man is determined by the month that he was born in. What??!!! I couldn't believe what I was hearing!! They were talking about how to get and keep a man!! Sad to say they were bragging about what all they did for their man and not the other way around!! One of the young ladies even mentioned that her mother was her partying and drinking buddy. It was so heartbreaking as I listened to single mothers who had children to raise main conversation be about men!!

How he likes for her hair and nails to look. The different types of food he loves instead of the kinds of food she and her children love. The young ladies appeared to be very submissive to men that they were not even married to!! So many women are in the same predicament, they fail to realize that they are the prize because they don't know their value!!!!! And because many women no longer know their self-worth, their children are suffering, and their future generations will also suffer. The scarceness of men has affected women so badly that we are the ones who are bending on one knee asking for the man's hand in marriage in fear of being a disgrace.

The word of God says, *He who finds a wife!!!!* Not she who finds a husband!!!

It's not your problem that there is a shortage of men- it's completely out of order to play the role of a man!!! Women have become so independent in the world in leadership roles, in politics, and in the work force that the enemy has confused us to thinking that we are the head in our marriages and relationships. You may be strong, but you weren't designed to provide for the man, he was designed to provide for you!! There was a time that men knew if he wanted a woman, he had to at least have a job and a car!!! Nowadays, it seems to be ok if he doesn't because women have lowered their standards so low that a lot of men no longer strive hard to pursue or please a woman because he knows he doesn't have to. Sad to say, many women are striving to please a man!! In the Bible, Jacob who loved Rachel agreed to work 7 years in exchange for her hand in marriage. After he had toiled 7 years, he was given the older sister Leah. But because he was so in love with Racheal, he agreed to work 7 more years just so he could be with her. In all, he worked a total of 14 years to be with the woman that he was in love with.

Racheal didn't pursue him, he pursued her!!

When a man truly loves you, he will pursue you-you don't have to pursue him!! He will put forth an effort to be in your life and to make you happy. You don't have to chase after a man, if he wants you, he will chase after you!! When we as women understand who we are men will respect us more. More and more women are playing the male role while some are unashamedly taking on the female role. And because we don't know our value, many men are saying *"what one woman won't do for me another one will."*

Instead of us standing firm with boldness and confidence seeing ourselves as God sees us, we fall in the trap that the enemy uses against us and we compromise because we are afraid of being alone. So many women have put their lives and the life of their children in harm's way by being involved with a man that they knew wasn't right for them.

But because they didn't want to be alone, they sacrificed their lives. There are women who works 2 and 3 jobs while the man stays at home- And to top it all off, drops her off at work and picks her up in her car. The roles have changed tremendously!!! Instead of men taking care of women, women are taking care of men!!! She has no clue about what God says about her.

She doesn't understand how special she is!!

Working as a nurse for 20 plus years, I have witnessed so many heartbreaking stories. There were women who refused to leave abusive relationships because they believed that their man was showing them love by beating them. Women who felt life wasn't worth living after a breakup. As well as women who have given up their children to be with a man who was molesting them.

So many women have lowered their standards so low due to fear of being alone. Many women feel that they are worthless if they are man-less. That woman doesn't know her value or her self-worth. She has been convinced that something is wrong with her and that she's a failure because she's not married. So, she eagerly gets married and regrets it, but she would rather live in misery than to be alone. Sad to say, she doesn't understand her value nor her self-worth. Woman of God, if you feel that a man is not pursuing you strong enough, the absolute and legitimate reason is the fact that he's not into you. It's ok!! He's not the one- just move around!! A part of a man's manhood is to be the chaser, the initiator in relationships. If he's interested in you, no distance and no one will stand in his way. The moment you realize someone isn't interested in you and playing games with you go the other direction!! Don't waste your time pursuing someone who only wants to play with your mind, feelings and your body. Your value is far above rubies. God will bring someone into your life who is truly and genuinely interested in you. Woman of God it is imperative that you understand how special you are!!

Women are so special that God used a "woman" to bring Jesus into the world to destroy the works of the enemy.

Gen 3:15 says – *"And I will put enmity between thee and the woman, and between thy seed and her seed: it shall bruise thy head, and you shall bruise his heel."*

Because God used a woman to bring Jesus into the world, Satan is angry with women. And that is why women are always under attack.

She's attacked in her body, her mind, her relationships you name it. Her attacks are greater because the enemy knows that she is the carrier of the seed of righteousness, and the carrier of the future. The enemy will use anything to destroy a woman, but he typically uses men.   A Woman's desire is to be loved and protected, but the enemy has used men vigorously to hurt her and to destroy her destiny. Satan knows that if he gets a woman depressed, desperate, lonely, anxious and etc.... chances are everything in her life will go wrong. The children will not be raised   properly, the man will not stay focused, the entire household will be out of order which poses no threat to the kingdom of darkness. The enemy's desire is for women to be powerless, for her to never know her value and self-worth and to yield to everything that is contrary to what God has already said about her. When we understand how valuable we are, we won't yield to the schemes of the enemy. We will be victorious women of God who will lead, guide and instruct other women and our future generations. When you understand your value and your self-worth and walk up-right before your children, they will rise and call you blessed!! It's very important that you understand how valuable you are because if you don't your daughters won't either!!!

Allow God to change how you see yourself and allow Him to mold you into the woman that He desires for you to become no matter how long it takes. You're everything that God has said that you are. You are perfect and complete in Him. He wants you to know that you are a special, worthy, and valuable woman, and no matter what situation you are currently in - He loves you!!

2 EMBRACING YOUR SINGLENESS

Being single can be tough but it's better than being in a bad relationship. There are severe consequences when we marry the wrong person. It's ok to desire to be married, marriage is an awesome thing and It's honorable in the sight of God. The problem is when we don't consult God before marriage or take heed to the warning signs. Being single is a great time for you to learn who you are, to build and enhance yourself. There is an assumption that singles are lonely, miserable, and desperate to get married and in a lot of cases, it's true. Joyce Myers once made a statement that, *"Married people are mad and single folks are sad."*

Many single people have an assumption that marriage will solve their problems and find out the truth once they say I do. The enemy has whispered lies to many single women that they're not whole and complete unless they have a spouse or a companion, but you must be whole and complete before you get married and that comes from having the Joy of the Lord. You can have joy as a single person and maintain it forever because it comes from God. Whenever you look to someone else to bring you joy then it will be difficult for you because joy is one of the fruits of the spirit, it's the result of having the indwelling of the Holy Spirit so it remains no matter what. No one can bring you joy like your Heavenly Father!!

Nehemiah 8:10- says- "The joy of the Lord is your strength" –

Many are looking to marriage for happiness. What if you never get married? That's why it's important to obtain joy married or not. Joy is when you make peace with who you are, why you are and how you are. You must have joy before you get married. You can have joy knowing that your father truly cares about you and loves you.

Jeremiah 17:7. Says- "Blessed is the man that trusteth in the Lord, and whose hope the Lord is."

Our hope has to be in God not man. Being truly happy is when you put your trust in God. Many singles think that being married will make them happy. They miss out on the joy and the advantages of being single because they spend most of their time depressed because they're not married. Being single can be the best time of your life if you take advantage of it. Most of us never picture ourselves being single for a long time but it happens and it's happening more and more. Do not allow being single stop you from living a good life, stop you from purchasing that dream house or car, or from starting your business. Do not place your life on hold waiting to get married. The time to pursue everything your heart desires is while you are still single.

There are so many women who are so saddened that they're not married, that they'll settle even if they don't benefit from it. They just want to be able to say that they are *"married."*

Isaiah 4:1- says "In that day seven women shall take hold of one man, saying, We will eat our own bread, and wear our own apparel: only let us be called by thy name, to take away the reproach." Well, *"that day"* is upon us.

Here in America, there is such a shortage of men that women are feeling more and more that they are in a hopeless situation and they will do anything to keep from being in the category of the "unmarried." The enemy has come to make many single women feel hopeless and instead of her embracing her singleness, empowering and developing herself, she spends her time sad and depressed because she's still single. Woman of God, build and invest in yourself as well as acquire as much as possible!!

Ask yourself, "Do I want to wait until my spouse comes before I build a home, travel the world and enjoy my life?" "What if it's 5, 10, or 20 years later before I get married, will I put my life on hold waiting for marriage?"

It's not a guarantee that you will have a knight and shining armor to come and rescue you. Pursue those things that you desire, you have so much to offer yourself and others!! Make the best of your life. Never feel like you are worthless and have nothing to offer because you are single, your voice is waiting to be heard. *Because you are single doesn't mean that you don't have an impact on someone's life.*

Embrace your singleness while you wait for marriage. Understand that God can make your life great no matter what your status is. Enjoying your singleness is a sign of emotional maturity. *Philippians 4:11, Paul said, "I have learned that in whatsoever state I am, to be content."* The word content means in a state of peaceful happiness, to satisfy.

As you commit your ways unto the Lord, He will satisfy you in your singleness and all of your needs. Satisfy means to meet expectations, gratify, appease, pacify, to fulfil one's desires or needs. God knows how to satisfy you while you are in a state of singleness.

Wait on God for your spouse-

There are great blessings when we wait on God. And there are major repercussions when we don't wait on God. Majority of the problems we encounter is due to the fact that we didn't wait on God especially when it comes to our spouse. Some of us didn't know to consult God for our spouse and some of us disobeyed GOD. We ignored all the stop signs, and the people who tried to tell us better. And for whatever reason, many have suffered much heartache and headache. Many times, we go from person to person trying to land the right one when all God wants is for us to pray and wait on Him. Waiting on God can seem like forever, but trust His timing, He knows what, when, and how to bring it to pass. When we get tired of waiting, we get ahead of God and we error. You may have been waiting seems like forever but God hasn't forgotten about you. *"It's better to wait long than to marry wrong."*

Because I didn't seek God before I got married, I suffered great consequences. Not only did I suffer but my son suffered as well. Raising a child alone was one of the hardest assignments I ever faced, but God entrusted me with a wonderful son. And my number one priority was to raise him to be a man, not chase after one!!

The struggles of being a single parent has its own tough challenges and the commitment of never giving up makes you strive every day to be the best parent in the world. Yes, it's tough, and at times very exhausting!! It's only you and you're trying to figure out which way to turn, what to do and how to do it. I was always struggling to make ends meet and sometimes the ends would never meet. It was always something, as a matter of fact, if it wasn't one thing it was another!! Raising a male child alone, I had to be nurturing like a mother and tough like a father. Having to play both roles was very overwhelming at times. With no one to talk to, and no shoulder to cry on. I thought God had abandoned me!! I thought God was severely punishing me!! The more I struggled as a single parent, the angrier I became for marrying the wrong person!! At the time I couldn't see that God was going to turn my situation around as well as use me to be a testimony to other single mothers. All I could see was me, a single mother struggling trying to keep it all together. I allowed my temporary struggles caused me to feel like living a good life was totally impossible!!

Woman of God, you may have made many mistakes, had children out of wed lock, married the wrong person, or whatever wrong thing you feel that you have done. Just grab a hold to this one thing, it's nothing that God can't change! God knows how to turn your situation around!! In spite of all the mistakes you have made, God will turn things around for your good, but you must be willing to wait.

When you allow God to develop you there is a period of waiting, some longer than others but you must wait.

Isaiah 40:31- says – "But they that wait upon the Lord shall renew their strength; they shall mount up with wings as eagles; they shall run, and not be weary; and they shall walk and not faint."

While you are waiting – wait with expectations!! Waiting anxiously wears you out. It's natural to become anxious while you wait, but when you trust God's timing faith creates an attitude of expectation!! Some of us have prayed long and hard for a spouse and when it seems as though it's never going to happen, we stop expecting. We think that God hasn't heard our prayers, but He has heard every prayer that you and I have prayed. When we wait with a spirit of expectancy God is always behind the scenes working everything out. Be busy while you wait. Don't sit around twirling your fingers while you're waiting on the promises of God. Being busy and enthusiastic is way more beneficial than sitting around doing nothing thinking that someone is coming to rescue you. Make good use of your time by being involved in things that will improve your life.

1 Timothy 5:13 says- "Besides, they get into the habit of being idle and going about from house to house. And not only do they become idlers, but also busybodies who talk nonsense, sayings things they ought not to."

When you're productive you don't have time for foolishness. Women and men who spend their time doing nothing never pursue the greater nor do they fulfil their destiny. It is said, "that an idle mind is the devil's workshop." There's greatness on the inside of you!!! Self-Development is imperative!! Use your energy to build yourself and discover who you are and your abilities. Allow wisdom to lead and guide you and If you lack wisdom ask God for wisdom!!

James 1:5 says- "If any of you lack wisdom, let him ask God, that give them to all men liberally, and up braideth not, and it shall be given him."

God is always there to help you to better yourself. You will be very proud of yourself for not wasting time in your waiting season. You will never regret investing in yourself and living a productive and fulfilling life. You will be pleased with your achievements and happy about your accomplishments. And no matter how long you've had to wait, whatever God has promised you it shall surely come to past!

3 OVERCOMING LONELINESS

Loneliness is the state of being alone and feeling sad about it. It's a feeling of sadness or even anxiety that occurs when one is without company. Loneliness is an unpleasant emotional response to isolation. Loneliness is a feeling- so therefore we can choose to be alone and depressed or we can choose to turn our loneliness into having intimate time with God. When you are single and feeling sad because you desire a companion, it can lead to a state of depression. Oftentimes it's easy to grow weary in the wait, but God wants you to remain patient. Even in your loneliness, God has you on His mind.

Isaiah-41:10 says – "Fear not, for I am with thee; be not dismayed, for I am thy God. I will strengthen thee; yea, I will help thee; yea, I will uphold thee with the right hand of my righteousness."

God knew that there would be times that we will feel alone so He let us know that we don't have to be fearful or anxious, He is with us. When you are weak, He will strengthen you. And when you are in want of friends, He will forever be your friend, your best friend!! He is our Comforter, our Protector, He's our redeemer!! Our friend!!

We have all dealt with loneliness at some point, some more than others.

It's a familiar feeling for almost everyone.

Loneliness is a painful feeling that can take root deeply in you if you don't resist it. It's a feeling of being disconnected from humanity. It can cause one to have a sense of worthlessness and hopelessness. Loneliness has been known to be the death of many. People deal with loneliness in many different ways. Many people run from loneliness by hiding themselves away from the world while others may turn to excessive drinking, substance abuse, or binge eating. Many even go from relationship to relationship. Whereas I am an introvert by nature and being alone to myself is a norm for me, another person may be severely depressed. Me spending time to myself is a must – I always find a way to be alone with just me. Even when I have company it's imperative that I find a way to have some "metime." But to someone else having company at all times is necessary.

Being alone is not the same as being lonely. You can enjoy the company of yourself and not be sad and depressed. As a matter of fact, you can have the same joy being to yourself as if you were with someone because happiness and joy are not predicated on you having someone in your life. So, *if you think that your loneliness will be cured by having a companion you will always be lonely.* Loneliness can be defined as sadness because one has no friends or company, feelings of abandonment, rejection, and depression. Single people who suffers with loneliness believes that being lonely comes from not having a spouse/companion but there are many lonely married people. Many married people feel lonely, sad, and depressed as well. Marriage can't take away the feeling of loneliness because it's a choice-feeling - it's subjective. When you are single you often see couples showing affection towards one another and if you don't choose to have joy, depression will slowly begin to take root. You will begin to imagine yourself in romantic relationships and friendships, thinking that if you find the right person you will never be lonely again. God is the only one who can fulfill that void of loneliness in your life. He's our only guarantee, He is forever!!! And even though you may be waiting on God to send your spouse, you never have to feel lonely, God is with you. You may be alone, but you don't have to be lonely.

Feelings of loneliness can turn into fear of loneliness.

Fear of loneliness causes one to stay in unhealthy relationships.

So many are willing to spend time with people they really don't enjoy because they are afraid to be alone. It's more prevalent among women than men. Many women have even become mothers to protect themselves from being alone. But you are never alone when you learn how to connect with God.

God is the only one who can fulfill your void fully and completely. He provides comfort, gives us strength, courage and boldness to endure feelings of loneliness. As long as your Heavenly Father is with you, you're never alone.

Here are a few pointers for dealing with loneliness

Become active in your local church - Getting involved in your local church will keep you busy. When you're busy in the House of God you would less likely get lonely and depressed. If one does not serve the Lord as a single when they are available- it is highly unlikely that serving in the house of God will be a vital part of their married life. When you are single you should have only one goal- to serve God with your entire being. Serving God with your entire being challenges you to refuse to dwell on what life might be in the future- whether it is a life of unrestricted service to our Lord or marriage. What we do now matters!!! Don't wait until you're married to help build God's house.

1Corinthians 7:34 NIV says-.... An unmarried woman or virgin is concerned about the Lord's affairs. Her aim is to be devoted to the Lord in both body and spirit. But a married woman is concerned about the affairs of this world -how she can please her husband."

So, while you are waiting for your spouse, help build God's house and who knows, your mate may just find you in the house of God!! When you are busy about your Father's business, loneliness will not be your portion.

Join the Singles Ministry – Many churches have a *Singles Ministry* - not so you could find a spouse but so you can mingle and connect with other Christians and grow in every area of your life. You will be empowered as you surround yourself with other like-minded Christians. Some singles ministries travel, go to movies, concerts, have dinners and parties which allows you mingle and meet new friends. It's very important that you hang around other singles with the same mindset and beliefs. When you're weak they'll be strong for you and vice versa.

Seek a meaningful relationship with God – We weren't made to be lonely we were made to have a relationship with God. The one thing that can bring you out of loneliness is the connection we were made to have and that is our connection with God. Fall in love with your Father!!! Your relationship with God can fulfill all of your needs. When you seek Him, you will experience His love for you. The word of God tells us in *Matthew 6:33- "But seek first the kingdom of God and His righteousness, and all these things shall be added to you."* God knows what you have need of and He will give you the desires of your heart, but you must first seek after Him. *James 4:8a- says, "Draw near to God and He will draw near to you."* Your fulfillment is not in people or a person it's in God.

Go to college, take up a trade- learn a hobby - Stay busy!!! Remember your life doesn't stop because you're not married. There's still more to life!!! There's more to you!!! Don't waste your life waiting for someone and you fail to pursue your dreams and passion. Be proud of yourself by taking this time to improve yourself.

Spend time with family and friends – Holidays and Birthdays can be a very depressing time for many people. Not having someone to spend special days/occasions with has led many to suicidal thoughts and depression. As you spend time with your family you will find joy in being around your family and friends. Enjoy the people that are important to you. Never feel like you are worthless because you don't have a companion to share special occasions with. If you have children, enjoy them, they are a product of you. Never feel like your family isn't complete because you don't have a spouse, you have your children and they have you. Value your children, they have a way of making us feel special in their own way. You will find joy in celebrating meaningful moments with them.

There are many blessings that comes from a state of loneliness.

Loneliness is a reminder of the cross. *Matthew 16:24-25- says- "Then Jesus said unto His disciples, If any man will come after me, let him deny himself, and take up his cross and follow me. For whosoever will save his life shall lose it: and whosoever will lose his life for my sake shall find it."*

Allow your season of loneliness to be the tool to draw you closer to God, to develop an intimate relationship with Him. When you are lonely and need someone to talk to you always have God!! He'll never leave you nor forsake you, you're never alone!!

Love the Lord with all your heart, seek His face, read His Word, and share His love with others, and the spirit of loneliness will fade away. As you focus on a relationship with God and not on the things of this world, loneliness will not be your portion.

4 SELF-LOVE

The strongest action a woman could have is to love herself. When a woman loves herself, many get it confused thinking that she's uppity and boujee. It seems to be a problem if a woman loves herself and a problem if she doesn't. But self-love is necessary!! A woman who loves herself builds her own world. She understands that in order for her to love someone else, she must first love herself. When you love yourself, you won't allow anyone to treat you less than the queen that you are. A woman who loves herself refuses to please others at the expense of her emotional wellbeing. The more she loves herself the less foolishness she will tolerate. Woman of God, you must learn to love yourself!! Put forth an effort to practice self – love even when no one is around. Loving yourself means appreciating yourself.

Do not resist what makes you happy!! Go out even if you have to go by yourself!! Go shopping, get a massage, get your hair done, pamper yourself!! You are always with you so you might as well enjoy yourself!!! Treat yourself to a movie, go to that play or concert. You don't have to go on a date with anyone to enjoy yourself, learn to have fun by yourself!! If you are an adventurous person, travel and explore

SINGLE, SATISFIED & SET APART

the world. If you don't have friends to tag along go by yourself. When you love yourself, you don't need the validation of others.

To love yourself means to love yourself regardless of your past, regardless of your flaws - without apology.

When you love yourself, you won't be satisfied with anything less than what God has for you!!! Loving yourself means turning your back to stupidity!!! Just because there is a shortage of men doesn't mean that God has forgotten about you, so you don't have to settle. Your Heavenly Father will send you a real man, someone who will love you and add to you. Not someone that you will have to take care of. Taking care of a man is a sign that you love him, but he doesn't love you.

Quote- "A woman can't change a man because she loves him, a man changes himself because he loves her." If he truly cares about you, without a doubt he will provide for you, there's no limit.

When you love and respect yourself, you don't have to tell anyone because it is very obvious. You know how you're supposed to be treated and you will not succumb to anything less. When a woman struggles with loving herself, it's very hard for even the right man to love her, and the wrong man will abuse and take advantage of her. The wrong man will degrade and disrespect her and she will accept it because she has belittled her own self. He causes her to think that she needs him but instead he needs her. He convinces her that he is the prize because she doesn't know that she is. The wrong man creeps in this type of woman's life because she doesn't require anything from him, she's just happy to say that she's married.

Isaiah 4:1 -KJV- And in that day seven women shall take hold of one man, saying, "We will eat our own bread, and wear our own apparel: only let us be called by thy name, to take away our reproach."

This is not what you call self-love. There are many women who are willing to settle because there is a shortage of men. They don't care if he's not loyal to them, if he doesn't love them or care about them as long as they can say they are married. They're afraid of being alone, and afraid of what people will think of them. They anxiously marry and live a miserable life and provides for someone who is supposed to provide for them. Women, we are the prize! I know that we are in this new age, but the prize for a man is the woman!! The Bible says, He who finds a wife, not she who finds a husband!!! God said her price is far above rubies not his! Women you are the prize!!! There once was a time where the man chased the woman, now a lot of women have become the chaser!!! No longer are the older women teaching the younger women.

Titus 2:4-5 says- "That they may teach the young women to be sober, to love their husbands, to love their children. To be discreet, chaste, keepers at home, good, obedient to their husbands, that the word of God be not blasphemed."

There are many older women who are not an example to younger women. Many older women feel that they're in a hopeless situation themselves so they can't instruct the younger women. God has placed a desire in every one of us to love and to be loved and when you love yourself you will find contentment while you are waiting for your spouse. Yes, we all want a companion/spouse, but it should not be to the extent that you settle. Love yourself so much that you would rather be by yourself if you're not treated like the queen that you are!! Love yourself so much that if no one ever comes along you're ok with being by yourself because you are loved by your Heavenly Father. When you love yourself, validation from others is a bonus. You will aim to look good and smell good if no one ever complements you. Self- Love will cause you to improve yourself for you! You will look good for you! Smell good for you!!! Lose weight for you!!! You can't truly love anyone else without truly loving yourself!! Invest in yourself!! You do not exist just to please others; you exist for yourself first!! You weren't created just to make man happy and neglect your own happiness. How can you make anyone else happy and you don't even make yourself happy?

Love the way God made you: Psalms 139:14- says, I will praise there for I am fearfully and wonderfully made: marvelous are thy works; and that my soul knoweth right well."

We live in a world that makes women believe that if she's not perfect she won't fit in and will not be accepted. Where television paints a picture that women must have the perfect face, hair, and body. The image that is portrayed on television has affected many women in the way that they perceive themselves. It has caused so many women not to feel good about themselves because of their size, the color of their skin, their hair and etc. So, they struggle with loving themselves and accepting who they are.

Woman of God, God has already declared that you are fearfully and wonderfully made!!! When God made you, He didn't make any mistakes!! He loves you just the way you are!! You are the "apple of His eye" – you are special to Him. If we are honest, we all have something about ourselves that we don't like including the ones who are painting a perfect picture. But regardless of how you feel, you're still worth loving and you have a lot to offer yourself and the world!! Don't allow your flaws to hinder you - we all have them. Count your blessings because many people are laid up in a hospital bed who would love to have your dark skin or white skin that you hate. They would love to have your big eyes or beady eyes you despise. Your kinky or straight hair that you're always complaining about, someone would love to trade places with you!! Be grateful and count your blessings!!! When God made you, He didn't make any mistakes, "you are fearfully and wonderfully made!"

Never compare yourself to others!!! *Galatians 6:4 says- Each one should test their own actions. Then they can take pride in themselves alone, without comparing themselves to someone else."*

When you compare yourself to others you will not focus on your own strengths and abilities. Comparison puts your focus on everything except what's really important and causes you to lose focus. Instead of you focusing on areas that are important and need improvement you'll start feeling that you don't qualify or fit in and stop fulfilling your dreams and desires. *Comparing yourself with others will rob you of your joy!!*

Some of the people you are comparing yourself with are sometimes pretending!! Sometimes they don't have any more than you do!! As a matter of fact, you may have more than they have!! Sometimes the people you are comparing yourself with aren't even authentic, what some of them are doing is copying from someone else and making it look very glamorous. We find ourselves impressed with people who knows how to make nothing look like something. There is a saying that, *"The Grass isn't Always Greener On the other side of the fence."*

Don't be fooled by what you see because it could very well be a façade. In other words, looking at someone else life, it appears that they're in a better situation than you, but in actuality, they're not. Comparing yourself with someone else will cause you not to appreciate your own accomplishments. We compare ourselves to others because we're not satisfied with our life and when you're not satisfied with your life you will always assume that someone else's life is better. The spirit of comparison is so dominant that it has affected people in every area of their lives. Parents are comparing their children to someone else's children. Children are comparing their parents to their friend's parents. Wives and husbands are comparing their marriages to other married couples. Many people are comparing their homes and cars to their family members, friends, and neighbors because they're never satisfied with what they have.

When we compare ourselves with others it causes us to be ungrateful to God. Paul said in *Philippians 4:11 KJV- "Not that I speak in respect of want: for I have learned, in whatsoever state I am, therewith to be content."*

The word content means in a state of peaceful happiness. It doesn't mean to stay in the same spot you're in forever, it means to be satisfied with where you're at -at the moment.

God wants all of us to increase and to go from glory to glory, but he doesn't want us to go ahead of Him. Everything has its own timing.

Ecclesiastes 3:1 says – To everything there is a season, and a time to every purpose under the heaven.

If you go ahead of time looking at what others are doing, you will not succeed. Wishing to be like someone else without knowing all the details has caused many to error and fall. Many of us desire to be like people who have mastered faking their way through life. There are also many people who have worked hard and who have truly paid the price to be great. Either way, we should never try to be like anyone else!! Striving to be like someone else and comparing yourself to others will always cause many problems in the long run. It will eventually lead to competitive jealousy and envy.

When you wait on God you can rejoice and be happy for others. It may not feel good but wait your turn, everyone gets a turn. Many are trying to make a name for themselves and make their name great. No!! God said He'll make your name great!!! When God opens doors for you no one will be able to shut them. Most of us don't want to start from the bottom, we just want to jump out there and be great. "No one starts on top except the ditch digger." Instead of comparing yourself to others, take advantage of where you are now and prepare yourself for something much greater.

Remember, if you go ahead of your time you won't succeed.

Never feel like a failure because of what others are doing, your time is coming. There are many who moved ahead of God and didn't succeed because it wasn't time, they followed others and failed. Whenever God is in the midst of your plans, you will succeed- no one said it would be easy but the anointing to succeed will be with you. When you love yourself, you are your own cheerleader!! You won't allow your joy to be taken by comparing yourself to someone else. You know that everyone has their own fears and weaknesses, yet you understand that you are a woman with power, purpose, and impact. You're authentic and no one can be you except you!! You are who God made you to be. God loves you!!! Give yourself permission to love yourself!

5 DISCOVER YOUR PURPOSE

Believe it or not, women also have a purpose and it's not just to have babies and help a man fulfill his purpose. When I was younger, I was surrounded by women who thought that a woman's job was to help their husband fulfill his purpose only. Even as a teen I have always felt some type away about this unbalanced belief. I would always ask myself, "What if he decides to leave?" Or, "What if something happens to him, then what?" Michelle Obama made a powerful statement. She said, *"it's important to become more than just someone's wife."* I totally agree with that statement. God has placed something great on the inside of everyone, and He has a plan just for you!! You were born for a specific assignment and purpose. May you discover your God's given purpose!!

Jeremiah 29:11 NIV says – "For I know the plans I have for you,"
declares the Lord, plans to prosper you and not to harm you, plans to
give you hope and a future."

The purpose of your life is greater than your own happiness, family, or fulfillment. To know why you were placed on this earth you must first start with God, your creator. You were born by his purpose and for His purpose. You were put on earth to make a contribution. Fulfilling your purpose will make an impression on someone or somebody. Many people never discover their purpose in life because they start with themselves. What do *I* want to be?

What are *my* dreams and goals?

By focusing on yourself, you will never discover your purpose. You didn't create yourself so therefore you can't tell yourself what you were created for. Many times, we are taught to focus on what we are good at and go from there. Yes, it may lead to great success but is that what God created you to do? You can reach all of your personal goals and never discover the purpose for which God created you. You may choose your spouse, your career, and etc... But you don't choose your purpose. You discover your purpose and identity through a relationship with God. You were created to serve God and when you serve others you serve God. You were saved to serve God.

The bible says, *"It is he who saved us and chose us for his holy work, not because we deserved it but because that was His plan."*

He's the one who planned out your purpose before you ever

44

existed. Your birth was not a mistake. Your parents may have not planned your birth, but God did. It doesn't matter what kind of parents you have, God needed their genetics to create you. You were on God's mind and He decided how you would be born; your race, the color of your skin, the color of your eyes, the texture of your hair and every other feature. You were on His mind and you are here today because God created you for His purpose. He determined when you will be born and how long you will live. God never makes mistakes!!!

The word of God says – *Psalm 139:15 MSG- "You know me inside and out, you know every bone in my body; You know exactly how I was made, bit by bit, how I was sculpted from nothing into something."*

He was thinking about you before He created the world. God created you because of His love. He is a God of love. *James 1:18-MSG- He brought us to life using the true Word, showing us off as the crown of all His creatures:*

When you know your purpose, it gives you a sense of well-being. It gives meaning to your life. Not knowing your purpose will cause you to feel like a failure. Without God, life has no purpose or meaning, and we all were made to have meaning. Life is easier when you know your purpose. Knowing your purpose will save you time, money, and stress. Many people are chasing their tails because they have yet to discover their purpose. Knowing your purpose motivates you - it produces passion. It causes you to be focused on that one particular thing than trying to fulfill so many other things. Knowing your purpose simplifies your life.

Sometimes we allow the wrong things to steer us and we are even steered with the wrong motives in mind. When you are driven to try to prove a point, or for the need for approval you will fail. You were born for God's purpose and no one else. We look at the accomplishments and possessions of others and we're inspired but headed in the wrong direction. To feel the need to prove or impress someone is a huge mistake!! Walking in your purpose causes the grace of God to come on you. Not only were you created for a purpose, but God will grace you to fulfill it. Have you ever seen someone walking in their purpose and it just appears to be so sweat-less? Well, that's because he or she has received grace to do it. And when someone else tries to do the same thing, they struggle and fail because if that's not their purpose they won't succeed at it. There's a special grace that comes on you when you began to walk in your purpose.

Sometimes we can't fulfill our purpose until we go through some painful experiences. God has chosen you for a specific task and your life will go through a series of tests and trials to prepare you for your God-given purpose. If we are to be used by God, the experiences that we want to hide are the very ones that God wants to use to help others. For God to use our painful experiences, we must be willing to share them and stop covering them up. Admit our faults, failures, and fears so that others could be set free and encouraged. Your purpose could very well be what God has delivered you from. We hardly ever see God's purpose for our lives in pain, failure, or embarrassment while it is happening. Extracting the lessons from your experiences takes time. Our experiences can leave us with shame and embarrassment to the point that once we have been delivered, we want to bury the past because it causes so much pain, but God wants to use your pain to revive others. God has a purpose behind every problem.

Revive means -to resuscitate, bring to life, bring back to consciousness; give new strength or energy to.

Discover your gifts and skills. There are many people who discovered their hidden talents late in life. What is your passion? Is it singing, playing instruments, playing sports, you won't know what you're good at until you try it. You will eventually discover what you're good at. Ask yourself what do I really enjoy the most? Can I see myself doing this for the rest of my life?

It was 15 years ago when I received my first prophetic word that God will use me to minister to women. And even though it seemed like it was never going to happen, it was more that God wanted me to encounter. There were many more challenges and experiences I had to stumble upon. God had to take me on a journey both spiritual and physical, place some things inside of me and take some things out of me. He took me on what I call a very lengthy process but a well needed one.

Even though you may know your purpose there is still a waiting period and sometimes it doesn't feel good to wait.

You know that God has called you to do great things and has revealed to you that your destiny is huge but yet you feel stagnated. And it can be very frustrating watching others fulfill their destiny not because you are jealous but because you don't see the manifestation concerning what God has said about you. It seems as though it will never come to past!! You may find yourself getting anxious because you are very aware that you're getting older, not younger!!

Woman of God, trust God's timing, wait on the green light from God. Your turn is coming, as a matter of fact, in this life everyone gets a turn- whether it's a mountain top experience or a valley experience, we all will get a turn!! God hasn't forgotten about you just wait on him. You may even be surrounded by people who says that by now you should be doing more than you're doing, but don't worry about the Naysayers, God knows what He's doing. So many people are going ahead of God, may that not be your portion. If you get ahead of God, you will error. Your time is not the same time as the next person. The length of your process may be totally different from others. God has a specific time to show up for you and He will show Himself mighty in your life when it's time. He will give you the wisdom you need and connect you with the right people.

A few years before I started writing this book, I told many people that I was going to retire early, travel, and do all the things I have always wanted to do. My plan was to sit back, cross my legs, and reward myself for all the sacrifices I've made as a single parent. In times past, I received many prophecies concerning my destiny over and over and over again. Well, many years went by and still there were no signs of what God had spoken about my life, so I practically gave up on fulfilling my destiny. I saw others fulfilling their destiny, but I saw no signs of what God had promised me. The enemy had me fooled thinking that if it hasn't happened by now, that it would never happen. Sad to say, I was all good with that. I was completely satisfied with not fulfilling God's plan for my life.

God began to speak again just when I became very complacent and started looking forward to an early retirement. He began to bring to the forefront of my mind about what He said to me years ago concerning my destiny. God began to stir up on the inside of me what He's placed inside of me. He showed me clearly that all of the oppositions, obstacles, and trials that I have endured were all part of the process. God spoke to me through dreams, visions, and through His prophets- letting me know that now is the time to do what I was chosen to do before the foundation of the world. He began to align me and connect me with my destiny helpers.

There are many rocky roads on your way to fulfilling your purpose but don't get discouraged, it's all part of the process.

When you get distracted and fall down, don't stay there, get back up- your destiny still awaits you!!! God hasn't changed His mind about you!! When you respond to your calling and things seem to be going in the opposite direction, as you seek Him, He will help you!! He never said it would be easy!! It doesn't matter how many mistakes you've made; God knows how to get you back on track. When you walk in your purpose you will make an impact on people directly and indirectly.

"The soul which has no fixed purpose in life is lost; to be everywhere, is to be nowhere." – Michel de Montaigne

6 FORGIVE THOSE WHO HAVE HURT YOU

To forgive means to stop feeling angry or resentful towards someone for an offense, flaw or mistake. It doesn't mean forgetting, nor does it mean condoning or excusing offenses. *Forgiveness-* is defined as a conscious deliberate decision to release feelings of resentment or vengeance towards a person or a group who has harmed you. Sometimes we think we could never forgive someone for the most horrible thing that they have done to us.

Colossians 3:13 says, "Forbearing one another, and forgiving one another, if any man have a quarrel against any: even as Christ forgave you, so also do ye."

*Forgiveness is an act of faith-*You must decide to forgive those who have hurt you. Whether it's from molestation, rape, murder, abuse, or whatever it may be, you must take a step of faith and start the process to forgive. The reason it's a process is because it takes time -it's easier said than done.

Mark 11:26- says- "But if Ye do not forgive, neither will your Father which is in heaven forgive your trespasses." In order to be blessed, you must let go of all hurt and disappointments. God will use the very thing that the enemy threw at you to break you to be a testimony for others.

Genesis 50:20 -NIV says- "You intended to harm me, but God intended it for good to accomplish what is now being done, the saving of many lives."

Sometimes it's very hard to think that something good can come out of something so bad. You may find it hard to believe that you are capable of being great because of the attacks that the enemy has thrown at you. The setbacks, pain, and failures came to forfeit the plan of God for your life, but you are more than a conqueror!!! What lies deep within you is greatness!!! God knew that the affliction and agony that came to harm you would push you into your destiny. He already knew the disappointment and the disgrace that you would face and that you would overcome everything that the enemy threw your way. If you allow God, He will turn your battles into blessings!!!

Psalms 30:11 – KJV says "Thou has turned for me my mourning into dancing: thou hast put off my sackcloth, and girded me with gladness;"

When I was pregnant with my son, I went through one of the most painful and awful times in my life. There was always something!!! I was considered a high-risk pregnancy – constant bleeding and in pain, always threatening to miscarry. I couldn't work, I was on complete bed rest and was always making trips back and forth to the Emergency Room. Several doctors informed me that my chances of carrying my child was very slim. Each hospital visit brought bad news. The doctors said there's no way that my son would survive and prepared me for the worse. But because of God's grace he held on. I endured a very hard pregnancy and to top it off, 12 days prior to delivery all hell broke loose in my home. My husband at the time had me put away from our house not even two weeks prior to delivering our son. The time I needed my husband the most was the time the enemy came and brought the biggest chaos ever!! The person who was supposed to protect me had the police to escort me from our home!! Angrily, I had to go back to live with my parents. I didn't have any money, diapers, clothes, blankets, absolutely nothing for my soon to be born child!!! And there I was: sad, depressed, confused and mad because I didn't ask for this!!!

All I could think about was how good my life was before my son's father came into my life!! I was working and attending college. I had my life all planned out and I was working towards achieving my dreams. I assumed I had met someone who would add to me not destroy me!! So, there I was, back to my parent's house. I felt rejected, abandoned and ashamed!! Just like that, my whole world was turned upside down!! The stress was so unbearable that my pregnancy was in danger all over again!! Right today I am very grateful to my parents who did everything to make sure that the delivery of my son was successful. Unfortunately, it wasn't!! A few days after we separated, I could no longer feel my son moving so I made a doctor's appointment. When my Dr. examined me, he couldn't detect my son's heartbeat. We panicked!! The doctor explained to me that he was under stress and told me to prepare to go to the hospital to be admitted. No heartbeat!! When I went back to my parent's house to get ready to be admitted in the hospital, I remember lying in my bed feeling hopeless, no husband and my unborn child wasn't responding. My anxiety went through the roof!!

I didn't know what I was going to do!!

Apparently, my mother called my husband because while I was

lying there he walked through the door. The minute he came and stood beside me, my son kicked and kicked as if he was waiting for his father to come!! This was such an amazing moment for all of us!! The baby is moving!! Prior to this, they couldn't even detect his heartbeat!! Now he's kicking like a PRO football player!!! It's amazing how the presence of a child's father makes a huge difference in the life of that child. The bible says, "the glory of a child is his father." When we informed the Dr. about what happened, it canceled out the emergency admission to the hospital, but a few days later I went into labor.

Due to the stress of my pregnancy, the delivery was very difficult. Bringing a child into the world under any kind of stress is very detrimental to the child's health. I felt "death" lingering in the delivery room, my vital signs were all over the place!! I was in a horrible situation!! I was in active labor for 30 hours!! Again, my husband was nowhere to be found, my mother had to go find him. As I laid there in the hospital bed I kept trying to figure out, "What caused all of this? "Is this a dream?" So many thoughts raced through my head as I was trying to figure it all out. *Why me* Lord? But In spite of it all, God saw fit for my son and I to survive the storm. I delivered a 7lb 16 oz baby boy. The hand of God was upon us!!

When a woman is pregnant there's usually a line called the linea nigra, or the pregnancy line on a woman's belly. This line runs vertical on the woman's belly. However, I had both- a horizontal and a vertical line that looked like a cross on my belly while I was pregnant. Everyone who saw it thought it was the strangest thing ever. For whatever reason it was there, still today I claim that the cross on my belly was a sign that the hand of God was upon the both of us. The doctors called my son a miracle child because they didn't expect for him to survive. From the time I found out I was pregnant all the way to the time of delivery, there was one problem after another one. But God kept us!!

After the delivery of my son, physically and mentally I suffered!! My Hormones were all out of whack!! I experienced depression at an all-time high, along with agony, distress, and excruciating pain!! I was angry, bitter, and filled with hatred towards my husband!! I was so angry I felt like killing him!!! My back was up against the wall and I didn't know how we were going to make it. I had no job, no money, a husband but no help. I found myself always thinking about my life prior to marriage compared to what it's like now. The overwhelming thoughts caused me to go deeper and deeper into depression. When my son was 6 weeks old, I felt like I was going to lose my mind- I couldn't eat, sleep, or think right. I couldn't take care of myself nor could I take care of him. It had gotten so bad I had to be admitted into a psychiatric hospital to get some help. This kind of humiliation couldn't be explained!! The heartache and shame that I endured made me feel worthless, and lifeless. How was I ever going to recover from such hurt, shame, and misery from my husband!!

After I got over the post-partum depression, my son and I stayed with my parents until I could do better. There were times I would reach out to my husband for help and he would joke about me being in a destitute situation. This type of hurt couldn't be explained. The hate kept building and building, and the more he allowed the enemy to use him to hurt me the more I hated him!! At the time I didn't understand that the enemy was using my husband to destroy my destiny and the destiny of our son. I also didn't realize how I was destroying myself by hating him. If I could be honest, I wished many days that someone would notify me and tell me that he was dead!! That's how much I hated my son's father!!! I hated him so bad that I attacked him every time I saw him! I went to jail once for fighting him, and almost went a second time. I knew that I was getting myself into a world of trouble, but at that time it didn't matter!! I hated him!!! I was so angry that I made a promise to myself that I would seek revenge if that was the last thing I did!! I Didn't know that I was hurting myself but "hurt people, hurt people." I knew what God said about vengeance, but I wanted to take matters into my own hands!! Some people told me that I needed to forgive him, and some said I should get revenge. I was angry and everyone knew it!! Because I hated him so much, it costed me money, jail, and almost cost my soul!! Eventually, I realized I couldn't live like this forever because I was only hurting myself. And needless to say, I was hurting my son.

The road to forgiveness:

I thank God for the ministry of Dr. Rick V. Layton in Shreveport, La. Dr. Layton taught us the importance of forgiveness and the danger of unforgiveness. This was a time in my life where I knew that I couldn't afford to miss not one church service because my life and my child's life depended on it. If I wanted a peace of mind, the only place that could help me was the church!! I was at a church where worship and the word of God began to break up my stony heart and little by little God began to change my heart. A part of me still did not want to forgive him but the word of God had been planted and had started to make an impact in my life. After hearing so many messages about unforgiveness, I was put to the test.

Just when I had made up in my mind to move forward with my life, one day, the Lord spoke to my spirit and said, "call him and ask him to forgive you." I said, "No Lord, I haven't done anything to him, he did me wrong!!" Again, God said, "call him and ask him to forgive you." And again, I said, "I haven't done him no wrong, he wronged me!!!" The Lord spoke to me the third time and this time I said, "Yes Lord!!" And of course, I did just that. When I called him, he was confused but I obeyed God!! For me to humble myself and ask him to forgive me and he's the one who put me out at 9 months pregnant and neglected his son!! Oh, that had to be God!! I went from hating him and promising myself that I would get revenge- to calling him asking him to forgive me. Oh, that had to be God!!

What a mighty strange feeling that came over me but what a mighty relief it was!! God wanted me to take on His spirit and not my own spirit. God wanted to bless my life and He knew that I had to take a step of faith and put to action what I had been taught so that He could bless me. God wanted to take me from glory to glory, but I had to learn how to forgive. Sometimes we have to apologize even when we haven't done anything wrong!!

2 Timothy 2:12a- says "If we suffer with him, we shall also reign with him"

Unforgiveness grows into bitterness and resentment, poisonous emotions that torture you. These emotions cause stress and pressure and can lead to unhealthy physical and emotional ailments. However, forgiveness calms stress, leading to improved health.

When you don't forgive, you're setting yourself up for disaster in every area of your life. Not forgiving someone who has hurt you stagnates you in every area of your life. The truth of the matter is, the person that you're holding on to has gone on to hurt someone else and is no longer thinking about you. And your life is in shambles while you're hating someone who has gone on with their life. On many occasions they will even get their life right, ask for forgiveness and go on and live a great life. And because you can't forgive, you are left behind, stagnated, carrying that load of unforgiveness. Yes, it hurts when you have been done wrong, but when you refuse to forgive it hurts you worse.

Luke 9:23- says "If anyone desires to come after Me, let him deny himself, and take up his cross daily, and follow me."

In order to be disciples of Christ we must learn how to forgive.

Luke 17:4- And if he trespasses against thee seven times in a day, and seven times in a day turn again to thee, saying, I repent; thou shalt forgive him. The NIV version says- even if they sin against you seven times in a day and seven times come back to you saying, "I repent," you must forgive them.

Harboring unforgiveness affects our health, mind, soul and even our destiny. Even for the sake of our children we must learn to forgive. When our children see us walking in unforgiveness towards others we are not being an example to them. Because I had a hard time forgiving my ex-husband, I would latch out at him in front of my son. I wasn't setting a good example, I was angry!! Little did I know, I was teaching him to be angry, and to hate his father!! My son growing up hating his father was the last thing I wanted!! It was enough that he had to grow up without him, and to teach him to hate him was way too much!!! I got to a point where I wanted us to get along for the sake of our son.

When God healed my heart towards my ex-husband, my son was relieved!!

No matter what, children hate to see their parents fight each other. As my son got older, he was constantly being let down by his father. Slowly, the spirit of unforgiveness started to creep up in his life. His dad not only disappointed me but he disappointed our son as well. More and more his father stopped coming around and the little that he was providing for him, that even stopped. When my son needed his father the most, he was nowhere to be found. He wasn't around for important events such as; his high school graduation, or major accomplishments. He failed to instruct him on becoming a man and was nowhere to be found even in emergency situations. There were times he would go months and months without even calling our son. He made so many promises that he didn't keep and to top it all off, he would sometimes only call on Father's Day. Did this bother me? Absolutely!! Was he looking for words of gratitude from us? Recognition? Appreciativeness? What made him call on Father's Day?!!!

But because God had changed my heart, I didn't talk about his father. I didn't want to add fuel to the fire. I began to use wisdom and I began to teach my son to love and respect his father. To never disrespect him and to always pray for him. When we criticize our children's father/mother in front of them, we are teaching them to hate them and we are creating a problem for ourselves.

We don't know the impact that we have on our children and we must be very careful about what we say and seek wisdom so that we don't further damage them. In spite of how you feel, never downsize the absent parent, the child will learn the truth soon or later.

After I made a promise to walk in love with my son's father I was tested on several occasions. No mother thinks it's ok for anyone to constantly hurt her children. When my son cried, I cried!! I watched my son stand by the door many days waiting on his father to show up only to disappoint him over and over again.

I knew this was a situation that only God could handle. It seemed to me that as long as I was acting crazy and out of character, I didn't have to worry about him lying to my son. As long as I was busting windows, cussing, and fighting, he was showing up at least here and there. But when I decided to do things God's way and walk in love towards him, he really disappointed my son. Even he knew that God had changed my life.

One day his father called and said that he was hungry, needed money, and was in a destitute situation. The enemy wanted me to think about all the times my son and I needed money, food, and etc. and he was nowhere to be found. I wanted to tell him no, but I knew that I was being tested, I gave it to him. As a matter of fact, it made me feel good!!

Proverbs 25:21-22 NIV- says "If your enemy is hungry, give him food to eat; if he is thirsty, give him water to drink. In doing this, you will heap burning coals on his head, and the Lord will reward you."

He was $40,000 behind in child support and because I knew his situation, I cancelled all of it. Yes, they called me crazy, but *"whom the Son sets free is free indeed!!"* I understood that if I show mercy, God will show me mercy. The best thing that could have ever happened to me was for me to learn how to forgive. To know that vengeance don't belong to me, it belonged to God!!

Woman of God, forgive so that your father may forgive you, so that He may be pleased with you. And if it's hard for you to forgive, ask

God to do spiritual surgery on your heart. That's what God had to do for me, I couldn't do it on my own. No, it's not something that'll happen overnight, it's a process and your Heavenly Father is willing to go with you every step of the way because He wants to bless you.

Unforgiveness causes the heavens to be shut over your life. But when you forgive, the heavens are open, and God can release blessings in your life. Make up in your mind that you're going to somehow, someway forgive the person who has hurt you. You must realize that holding unforgiveness will destroy your life!! It's not worth losing your life, your mind, your destiny, nor your soul. *Let it Go!!!*

7 FORGIVE YOURSELF

---

2 Corinthians 5:17 says – KJV- Therefore, if any man is in Christ, he is a new creature: old things are passed away; behold, all things are become new. The NIV says – Therefore, if anyone is in Christ, the new creation has come; The old has gone, the new is here! It doesn't matter what you've done, what matters now is that you are in Christ and you are a new creature. Forgive yourself because God has already forgiven you.

1John 1:9 says – "If we confess our sins, he is faithful and just to forgive our sins, and to cleanse us from all unrighteousness." Woman of God, confess, ask for forgiveness and believe that you are forgiven. Believing that you are forgiven is most people's battles. In their hearts, they really don't believe that they have been forgiven so they continue to carry around their past. They continue to down themselves and remain stagnated because it's hard to believe that God will forgive them for all that they have done.

Psalm 103:12- let us know that, *God has removed our sin from us as far as east is from the west.* East and west will never meet, God washes our guilt and cleanses us from our sins. When God forgives our sins, He puts it out of His mind, erases our shame, and redeems us. When we are forgiven, we are entitled to the promises of God.

Isaiah 1:18- says, "Come now, and let us reason together, says the Lord, though your sins are like scarlet, they shall be white as snow; though they are red like crimson, they shall be wool."

Your Heavenly Father wants to commune with you because He loves you. He doesn't see your past. He sees your future. He wants you to know that the Love that He has for you is like non-other. Man may love you conditionally, but your Heavenly Father loves you unconditionally. He wants to give you *"beauty for ashes"* - The ashes are the wounded parts of our lives, and the hardest wounds to turn to the Lord are the ones that we have done to ourselves. But God is saying, *"Allow me to turn those ashes into beauty!!"* He wants to make you a brand-new person, He wants to give you a new garment. He still wants to bless you!! He still wants to use you and make your name great!! Forgive yourself, for all have sinned and come short of the glory of God. Stop beating yourself up about your past!! Forgive yourself for the abortion, prostituting and all sexual immorality, hurting others, lying, stealing, addictions, and for everything that's contrary to what God says. Whatever you may have done in times past, with a sincere heart ask God for forgiveness and let it go. You're not perfect, you are capable of making mistakes- all were born in sin and shapen in iniquity. Whatever it is, Christ has already paid the price for it all you have to do is walk on in it.

Romans 8:1 says- There is therefore now no condemnation to them which are in Christ Jesus, who walk not after the flesh, but after the Spirit."

The definition of *condemnation* is an accusation or a scolding or punishment for a bad act.

You're no longer bound to sin -You're free!!! Stop carrying around unnecessary weight - you are forgiven!! The same way it takes faith to forgive others it also takes faith to forgive yourself. Sometimes we can forgive others for hurting us faster than we can forgive ourselves. Forgive yourself so that you can live again. Guilt is toxic!! The enemy loves to beat you with guilt and condemnation but you got to know that you have an *advocate with the father,* and He is touched with the feelings of your infirmities. He's touched by your weaknesses, He's touched by your challenges- He knows your greatest strengths and your greatest challenges, yet He loves you and will forgive you.

8 DEFEATING TEMPTATION

Temptation- is an urge or desire to do something, especially something you should not, it also refers to a wrong or forbidden pleasure that is enticing.

"It's not a sin to be tempted, Jesus was tempted. Temptation becomes a sin when you give in to it."

Temptation always begins with a thought. Replace that thought by turning your attention to something else. While temptation is Satan's main weapon to destroy you, God wants to use it to develop you. Every time you choose to do good instead of bad, you are growing in the character of Christ. Temptation starts in your mind. We think temptation lies around us, but God says it begins within us. The enemy is always whispering lies to us, "One time won't hurt, this will make you feel better, everyone else is doing it." It is his way of getting you to act on what you are feeling. He always offers you something that's contrary to what God's word says. And the closer you grow to God, the more Satan will try to tempt you.

The temptation that most singles face is sexual temptation. The sex drive is one of, if not the most powerful temptation of our human nature. A lot of single Christians feel that if they get married this will go away. Yes, it helps a lot, but sexual temptation will never go away. The best thing to do is to learn how to deal with it while you are single.

Society doesn't make sexual purity easy especially for Christian men. More and more they are faced with attractive, under-dressed women on a daily basis. Most men will go without food, water, and sleep to first satisfy their sexual desires. Unless there is a renovation of the mind this will always be a problem. This is why Paul instructed us, "do not conform to the pattern of this world but be ye transformed by the renewing of your mind" Sexual temptation can't be voided but it's up to you to flee it at all cost. And sometimes we feel that temptation is too overpowering for us to bear, but with the renewing of our minds, the power of the Holy Spirit and the truth of God's Word to help us, we will effectively resist temptations.

SINGLE, SATISFIED, & SET APART

1   Corinthians 10:13 –says, "There hath no temptation taken you but such as is common to man: but God is faithful, who will not suffer you to be tempted above that ye are able; but will with the temptation also make a way to escape, that ye may be able to bear it." When you are tempted, God will show you a way out to keep you from giving in.

Ways to deal with Sexual Temptations:

Avoid Tempting Situations - If you think that you are going to be tempted when going on a date bring someone with you. Someone who will not allow you to yield to sinful thoughts that comes to your mind. If you feel that having company late at night will cause you to be tempted, have a cut-off time for your company. If wearing certain clothes or undergarments will cause you to want to sin don't wear them.

2 Timothy 2:22 says- Flee also youthful lusts: but follow righteousness faith, charity, peace, with them that call on the Lord out of a pure heart.

The TLB- says -run from anything that gives you evil thoughts that young men often have, but stay close to anything that makes you want to do right.

Monitor what you allow to enter your ear gate and eye gate- Be careful about what you allow to capture your attention. Refrain from X-rated movies and videos. Guard what you see and hear. Change the

TV station. Satan is out to destroy the mind and he knows the eye gate is the entrance to the soul. If you know that looking and listening to certain things are your weaknesses refrain from doing it. Allowing the wrong things to get into your spirit will cause you to eventually act on it. Setting boundaries to protect yourself from being tempted will help you to avoid situations that you would later regret.

Don't feed your mind sexual thoughts- When our minds and hearts are occupied in the right place, sexual lust has little room to operate. Meditate on the word of God.

Philippians 4:8-NIV- says- Finally, brothers and sisters, "Whatever is true, whatever is noble, whatever is right, whatever is pure, whatever is lovely, whatever is admirable if anything is excellent or praiseworthy think about such things."

Think deeply about the word of God, the things of God, His goodness. You defeat bad thoughts by thinking good thoughts. "You overcome evil with good." Satan can't get your attention when your mind is preoccupied with the things of God.

Recognize what causes you to be tempted- Whatever gets your attention tends to temp you. Satan knows exactly what you like, and he will send it to your doorsteps!! If hugging the opposite sex causes you to be tempted, shake their hand. Many men and women find themselves tempted when hugging. If being alone with someone you're attractive to temps you - avoid it at all cost. It is up to you to recognize what causes you to be tempted

Ignore The Temptation- Ignoring a temptation is more effective than fighting it. When your mind is on something else, the temptation loses its power. When the enemy brings your way the very thing that temps you- look away. Turn your body and mind towards the word of God. The word of God tells us to "Resist the devil and he will flee." To resist means to battle against something or someone that is attempting to defeat you.

Connect with people of God who will encourage you and pray for you - When all else fails, find someone you can trust and who will hold you accountable. Sometimes we need someone in our corner that we can talk to about how we feel who will pray for us and encourage us. *James 5:16a -KJV-says – "Confess your faults one to another, and pray one for another, that ye may be healed."*

9 GOD WILL TAKE CARE OF YOU

Anxiety is at an all-time high in the life of many single women especially in the life of a single mother. A single mother trying to figure out how and what to do has led many to extreme exhaustion. One of the hardest challenges in the world is to be a single parent and it's even harder when you don't have enough finances. The thought of having to do it all by yourself without anyone's help is enough to deplete you!! So many countless times you have cried and have desired for someone to come along and help you. And even though time and time again God has shown you that He'll take care of you, many times you doubt him because the struggle seems to never end. You've cried out to the Lord, *"If I had someone to help me, things would be a lot better."* You have even prayed, *"Lord please send me someone, I need help!!"*

Ecclesiastes *4:9-10 NIV says, Two are better than one, because they have a good return for their labor: If either one of them falls down, one can help the other up. But pity anyone who falls and has no one to help them up."*

Oh how true this scripture is!! Many single women don't have anyone to rely on but God!! Our Heavenly Father is always our help in time of need. Sometimes it's tough when you're single and even tougher when children are involved. It's all on you!! You are mom, dad, the provider, the nurse, the cook, the mechanic, you name it!!!! You know that you can't fall because if you do everything around you will fall. Everyone is depending on you!! And in your mind lies many questions. How will I make up for the lost wages if I miss work? Who's going to take care of the family if I can't? The burdens that you carry are heavy, you know that failing is not an option and sometimes you find yourself caught between a rock and a hard place. What your children eat and where they sleep is 100% your responsibility. You know it is important that you work and provide for your children, you also know that it's crucial that you properly raise them. If you don't work enough you can't make ends meet, and if you work too much, trouble is waiting for your children.

It clearly states in *Proverbs 29:15 that a child left to himself will bring his mother to shame.* So, what do you do??

As a single mother, I was faced with so many obstacles, and not being able to work how I wanted to was one of them. Before I got pregnant with my son, nothing stopped me from working and getting what I wanted. However, after my son was born, every decision I made was with him in mind and at times my hands were tied. I could no longer work like I wanted to because raising him was my first priority. When you love your children, you make the proper adjustments so that your children won't suffer.

Trying to shake back after a terrible divorce - My son and I moved out of my parent's house and we moved into some Section 8 gov't Apts. Shortly after that, I got accepted into Nursing School. We survived off food stamps, welfare, WIC and every kind of government assistance that was available. I had to swallow my pride so that my son and I could receive the help that we needed. Receiving a welfare check was not only an insult but a huge slap in my face. The welfare check I received every month was only $123. I really struggled trying to make ends meet because I didn't have enough, I was limited. My son suffered with asthma and severe allergies and we spent many days and nights in the ER and in the hospital. Many times, we received no help from his father, but God always provided. So many times I wanted to give up, but LOVE wouldn't let me. A mother's love is pure, unconditional and strong. Her strength is like no other, as a matter of fact, she discovers her strength when she becomes a mother. She doesn't give up because she knows that her children are depending on her. The challenges I faced raising my son alone caused me to want to throw up my hands, but God proved to me over and over again that He was with us. God promises us in His word that *He'll never leave us nor forsake us.* And no matter what, God has always made a way for us!!

It doesn't matter what you go through understand that God is with you!

Isaiah 43:2 says- "When thou passes through the waters, I will be with thee; and through the rivers, they shall not overflow thee: when thou walkest through the fire, thou shalt not be burned; neither shall the flame kindle upon thee."

Yes, it is hard, but you have the Greater One living on the inside of you and He will help you. Sometimes we're so focused on who's not around we can't see who is around. The world has taught us to depend totally on man, but God wants us to depend totally on Him!! Not the system, or your Boo!! Our hope should always be in the Lord!! When God gives you a spouse, they could never replace God, your trust must always be in the Lord.

Psalm 33:20-22 says- "Our soul waiteth for the Lord: He is our help and our shield." For our heart shall rejoice in him, because we have trusted in His holy name." Put your trust in your Heavenly Father!!

Psalms 118:8 tells us- "It is better to trust in the Lord than to put confidence in man"

When you put your trust in God, He will provide for you!! He is Jehovah Jireh Meaning, "The Lord Will Provide" When we call on Him, He answers. He may not come when you want Him to but He's always on time!! I'm a witness that He will make a way when there seems to be no way!!!!! He is way-maker!! A bridge over troubled water!!! A good Father!! You don't have to compromise your walk with God. God knows how to provide for you better than anyone!! You don't have to settle for less God wants to give you more!!!

He wants to direct your path!!

Trust God and submit to His ways- *Proverbs 3:5-6 NIV saysTrust in the Lord with all your heart and lean not on your own understanding; 6. In all your ways submit to Him, and He will make your paths straight.*

God has a system in place and when you learn to do things God's way, He will do great things in your life.

Joshua 1:8 says This book of the law shall not depart out of thy mouth; but thou shalt meditate therein day and night, that thou mayest observe to do according to all that is written therein; for then shalt thy make thy way prosperous, and then you shalt have good success.

Your success is tied to your obedience to God's word. When we are out of sync with God, the struggle lasts forever!!! It never comes to an end!!

The importance of tithing- One of God's method of operation is tithing. The tithe is 10% of your income that you give to your church.

Malachi 3:10 says- bring ye all the tithes into the storehouse, that there may be meat I mine house, and prove me now herewith, saith the Lord of hosts, if I will not open you up the windows of heaven, and pour you out a blessing, that there shall not be room enough to receive it.

God has a plan already in place to bless you but in order for

God to reveal His plan for your life, you must walk in total obedience.

It doesn't matter how bad your struggle is, in order for God to bless you, you must become a tither. When you give your tithes and become a giver, God increases you in ways you can't imagine!! Sometimes we miss our blessings because we get caught up wondering where our tithes are going and in doing so we stop giving. When you tithe, you do it because you love God. You give it out of a willing heart. Tithing is a form of worship and an act of obedience. Tithing is for your own benefit and it should be given with pure motives. So many people don't tithe because there are so many wicked Pastors who have abused God's money, but God knows how to curse and bless at the same time. He will bless you for your obedience and curse them for their disobedience!! Give to God what belongs to Him and watch how He blesses you!! God wants to use you to break generation curses of lack and poverty in your family!!

When you allow fear to be an excuse for why you don't tithe, you're hurting yourself as well as your future generations. The Lord wants to take such good care of you that when you do get married it won't be because you were struggling and looking for a way out. People will have to admit that God has been good to you!! You may be single, but you don't have to struggle. You don't have to wait to get married to have the finer things in life. When you walk upright before your God, He will bless you in ways that will blow your mind and the mind of those around you. God will take care of you, but you must obey the principles of God.

When I started obeying God in the area of my finances, I began to see my life change. I became a tither and a seed sower. I came to understand that there are biblical principles in place concerning finances that only work if I work them. It didn't matter how much I prayed or how much I cried, until I obeyed the word of God concerning tithing and giving lack was my portion. I started tithing 10% of my welfare check which was $123/month and I tithed 10% of everything I received and gave offerings. When I obeyed God, doors began to open for me. I was blessed to go to nursing school where all of my expenses were paid in full. We were living in the hood in section 8 apartments, surrounded by drugs, gang bangers and only God knows what, but no hurt harm or danger came near us because God kept us safe. Because I started tithing when my son was a few months, when he got old enough to understand what lack was, I had already gotten pass the struggle because I was a consistent tither when he was an arm baby. God has always provided for us!! He has shown himself to be

Jehovah Jireh, our provider!

There are times when I look back over my life as a single mother, and I weep profusely because I'm grateful for how far God has brought me. I went from tithing off of 10% of a welfare check of $123 to tithing 10% of a 6-figure income all because of obedience. The word of the Lord is SURE!!!! The Lord desires to bless you in such a way that your children won't know what struggle is. Put Him to the test and watch what He will do. Be consistent in tithing, remember *consistency is the key to the breakthrough!!*

God is faithful!!!! 7 months after purchasing a new home for my son and I, the enemy attacked me with an infirmity. The scary thing was no doctor knew what was wrong with me. My labs showed everything was normal, but my body was saying otherwise. What was normal for everyone else wasn't normal for me. It had gotten so bad that my parents had to help me for almost a year. Being a business owner, I knew that if God didn't intervene for me that I would lose my business, home and everything else. My job was an hour away from home and my father drove me every day for almost a year back and forth because my energy level was so depleted. There was a major attack on my endocrine system which affected my thyroid and my adrenals. My doctor suggested that I take off work for an entire year!! I didn't have a year's worth of finances to cover my expenses so that was totally impossible!! I kept going to work knowing that somehow, someway God was going to see me through!! Weekly I received IV's and injections so that my glands will function properly. At times I didn't know how much poking and probing I could take!! There were times I felt so discouraged I wanted to give up!! I was going back and forth to the doctor struggling with fatigue and low energy for at least 4 years. I went from having an abundance and an overflow of finances to struggling to make ends meet. I was robbing Peter to pay Paul!! My savings went on Dr. visits and medical bills. And because God is so faithful, I didn't lose my house, car, or business. As a matter of fact, during this time, God added to me. During the 4 years of dealing with this infirmity, God supernaturally made provisions for me. He sent people my way to help me to weather the storm. He stayed true to His promises towards me. He rebuked the devour for my sake. He's faithful!! No matter what comes your way, He's faithful. He didn't say that it was going to be easy, but He said that He'll be with you. When you're on the mountain top or in the valley, He'll be with you and one thing about the valley experience, everyone gets a turn!!

The word of God says, *Psalms 34:19 – "Many are the afflictions of the righteous: but the Lord deliverers him out of them all."*

When you walk in total obedience to God and apply the principles of God in your life, even though you may experience hard times you will come out victorious!

10 DON'T LOOK BACK

Isaiah- 43:18-19 says- "Remember ye not the former things, neither consider the things of old. Behold, I will do a new thing; now it shall spring forth; shall ye not know it? I will even make a way in the wilderness, and rivers in the desert."

The word of God tells us not to dwell on our past because there is something greater that God has in front of us. In order to walk in newness of life, you can't live in your past!! Your past will only hold you back!! Nothing ever changes there!! Don't look back, you're going forward!!!

God has something greater waiting for you. Everything happens for a reason, keep your head up and look forward!! The only reason why you should look back is to see how far God has brought you. And now that you are past your past- God wants to do something new in your life. He wants to give you double for your trouble!! He wants you to be a testimony to many others. Your past influences you one way or another, for the better or worse-may you look forward to the good. Looking back on your past will cause you to miss what God has in store for you. Your past will destroy your future if you don't leave your past in the past. Forget about your past, you can't change it, it's done!! The only thing that is back there is pain, mistakes, headache, and heartache. Look forward to where there's strength and learned lessons. Even forget about the people who want you to stay stuck in your past by keep bringing it up. Your past is your past!! Your destiny will never be found in the rear-view mirror.

You will only waste valuable time looking back on your past.

The only thing you want from your past is valuable lessons.

Keep your eyes on the prize, there's a prize waiting for you.

Philippians 3:13-14- says, "Brethren, I count not myself to have apprehended: but this one thing I do, forgetting those things which are behind, and reaching forth unto those things which are before, I press toward the mark of the prize of the high calling of God in Christ Jesus.

The word press means to proceed, to reach forward, to push. Sometimes it's not easy moving forward especially when life has knocked you down over and over again. You feel stuck and can't move forward. But God has great things in store for you.

Isaiah 61:7 says – "For your shame ye shall have double; and for confusion they shall rejoice in their portion: therefore in their land they shall possess the double: everlasting joy shall be unto them."

When God gives you a new beginning, don't repeat the old mistakes. God wants to bless you, to give you beauty for ashes-the oil of gladness instead of mourning, and a garment of praise instead of a spirit of despair. The enemy wants to hold you in bondage and clothe you with shame because he knows that you were called to do great things. The songwriter fantasia sings a song "It was necessary" Woman of God it was crucial that you went through what you went through.

The word of God says in Genesis 50:20- "But as for you, ye thought evil against me; but God meant it unto good, to bring to pass, as it is this day, to save much people alive."

In other words, you had to go through what you went through so that you could reach back and help others, and what the devil meant for evil, God turned it around for your good. The devil thought he did something when he took you through that horrible experience. If he would have known that your agony would have caused you to rise up with power - rise up with an anointing and with greatness, he would have never ever messed with you!! You shall come forth and help deliver and set others free!! That terrible breakup/divorce that has caused you shame, feelings of neglect, feelings of rejection and abandonment, it was all so that you could help deliver others!! The hurt you experienced was so bad that it drove you to think that drinking, abusing drugs, selling your body and doing other things was the answer, God wants to use it to help others. The very thing that caused you shame is what God wants to use to help free others.

Romans 8:18-19- "For I reckon that the sufferings of this present time are not worthy to be compared with the glory which shall be revealed in us."

Even though what you went through was devastating it doesn't compare to what God is going to do through you and what you're becoming. The sufferings and disappointments came to mold you and shape you into a better person as long as you don't allow it to make you bitter. God has mighty things in store for you, but you got to let go of how bad things were and embrace your new future and the testimony that you gained from it. God will even place you in strange places and situations, a very unfamiliar type of environment in order to thrust you forward, but If you can't forget about your past and you revert back to what you're familiar with, you'll miss it. God wants to do something so great on the inside of you that it impacts your generations to come. He wants to take you from the Ghetto to the Getmore - from the out-house to the in-house- and from the back burner to the front burner!! And one of the requirements for you to get there is that you must forget your past in order to receive the blessings of God!!

There were times in my life where I allowed my past to cling on to me and weigh me down. Past hurts, failures, mistakes, and disappointments would always resurface at times when I thought I was healed from them. I hadn't completely moved forward from my past, I only suppressed it enough to move forward just enough to get pushed back again. Even though I had forgiven myself and the people who have hurt me, I still allowed my past to hold me hostage. I have also missed out on many great opportunities and relationships due to fear of repeating my past. Instead of focusing on what's ahead I allowed my past experiences to whisper loudly in my ears which hindered me from going forward.

Some of us are like Lots wife, we're in love with our past and can't imagine walking into our future of greatness because all we can see is what was. God has given us a way out, but we still want to hold on to our past. When we can't let go of our past and look back to the point of return it ends in destruction.

A sure sign that you're not healed of your past is when you revisit it when you feel some type of way. There's a saying that says, "it's not the future that you're afraid of it's repeating the PAST that makes you anxious.

The impact your past has on your present is extremely powerful!! Unless you learn how to reconnect your past to your future then your whole life may be impacted in a bad way. Your past will always be with you, it flows in and out your mind. It wasn't until I completely let go of my past before I started seeing God really move in my life. When I stopped looking back on my past, then I was able to see my future. My past could no longer hold me in captivity. I saw a new me and a new life. I began to leap forward because I stopped looking back.

As you press forward and enter into your wonderful future, remember you can't recover what happened yesterday, but the future is yours to gain.

11 GOD HAS SET YOU APART

God has set you apart!!! To be *Set Apart means -to make someone or something different and special. To select something or someone for a specific purpose or a specific task. Other words used to describe being set-apart are; to consecrate, dedicate, devote, reserve, save, isolate, or keep apart.*

Woman of God you are different!! God has called you by name for a specific purpose. That's why you can't fit in and do what others are doing. When God has set you apart, what others get by doing you will get caught!!! God has purposely allowed you to see that you can't do what everyone else is doing. There once was a time that you didn't know that you were chosen, you just knew that you couldn't get by like everyone else. Your friends may have gotten by walking in disobedience for years but the minute you start you get caught. Where others may have gotten by committing sexual sins when you start you get pregnant. It's because you're chosen and it's not until you mature in Christ that you'll be able to understand why you could never get by. *"For whom the Lord loves, He chastens."* The word chastens means to *correct, to punish, to discipline.* God loves you so much, He has His way of getting your attention. The chastening is not to scare you but to place you on the right path that God has designed specifically for your life.

2 Timothy 1:9 says- "Who hath saved us, and called us with a holy calling, not according to our works, but according to his own purpose and grace, which was given us in Christ Jesus before the world began."

You were called to do great and mighty exploits for Christ and if He called you, He will equip you. He has His hand on you so therefore you must live the life God requires you to live.

Many Christians don't want to be set apart/sanctified because of the desire to be accepted by the world. The clubs, the party life, hanging out and the freedom of feeling like *"I'm my own"* always seems to be more of a benefit but you are chosen!!!

The Word of God tells us in *Romans 12:2 -KJV- says- "And be not conformed to this world: but be ye transformed by the renewing of your mind, that ye may prove what is that good, and acceptable, and perfect, will of God."*

The word of God also tells us to "Be Ye Holy for I am Holy!!" So therefore, when God has called you, He requires you to live a life of holiness and sanctification.

I grew up in a *"Sanctified Church"* or should I say in the Church of God in Christ. When I was younger my impression of being sanctified was wearing dresses only, no makeup, no fingernail polish, and being able to speak in tongues. This type of belief has misled many in the wrong direction. Even though my mother was brought up in the "holiness church," she was totally against the dress code which was good for me because she didn't make my sister and I wear dresses all the time. But when I went around my family and friends who strongly believed in women not wearing pants, I can recall changing out of my pants into a dress or a skirt in fear of being criticized. I can even recall being around some of the saints who didn't wear pants nor makeup, but they lived like a heathen and cussed like a sailor. Some of them used to say that the benefits of wearing dresses was for *"easy access."* It was very confusing. I assumed that because the church folks approved of them that their lifestyle was pleasing onto God. This deception of sanctification has caused many in the Body of Christ to leave church and go astray. It wasn't until I matured in God that I learned that the heart is what matters when it comes to sanctification.

Loving and following God and doing what He tells you to do is what sanctification is.

Yes, Christians should dress appropriately, and I don't think there's nothing wrong with a dress code for church, but it does not determine a person's salvation or if a person is truly sanctified. So many people have been deceived because sanctification has been viewed as an outward appearance instead of an inner process. There are so many times where people have been turned away from the church because of the way they were dressed. Could you imagine turning someone away from the church who's on the verge of committing suicide? Or rejecting someone because they're wearing makeup?! God is more concerned with a person's insides, His main purpose for coming is for salvation not for a person dress code. You can't prove that you are sanctified by the way you dress. When God sanctifies you, everything about you will begin to change.

Sanctification is one of the greatest things that has and is happening to every believer in Jesus Christ. Sanctification doesn't stop with salvation it's a continual process whereby God brings change in our lives by means of the Holy Spirit.

We all face different issues, struggle with past hurts and sins that hinders our ability to live the life God desires for us. However, when the Holy Spirit comes into our life, He convict us in areas that needs to be changed. When we began to be Christ-like, we see life in a spiritual way instead of the natural way so therefore we're motivated to strive to live a life of purification and sanctification. Sanctification doesn't just come overnight it's a process and it's different for each individual. It's not about being sinless because we will never be sinless in this life. But it's for our very own benefit so that through it we may be blessed. As we put off the works of the flesh and take on the fruit of the spirit, we are made sanctified through Christ Jesus.

12 BUILDING A LEGACY

If we are honest, most of us just want to help our children become independent, get out of debt and save for retirement. The thought of building a legacy is far from most of our minds especially when you're a single mother. However, it is God's will that we build a legacy for our 'future generations."

Proverbs 13:22 – says "A good man leaveth an inheritance to his children's children: and the wealth of the sinner is laid up for the just.

A Financial Legacy-is when one leaves assets, real estate, savings, and investments to their heir.

Many of us were never taught to build a financial legacy for our children. As a matter of fact, the children had to help the generations before them. The burden that comes from being a single parent sometimes crushes the desire to build a financial legacy. Most of the time, it's the last thing on the mind of a single parent who is the provider, both mom and dad, the cook, chauffeur, counselor, nurse you name it!!! Your biggest desire is to help your children get to a point where they are totally independent so that one day you can take a break!!

Building a legacy is far from the minds of most married people, more so a single mother!!

Many women believe that in order to build a legacy that she must first be married. Many feel they should wait before they're married before excelling let alone build a legacy!! Time and time again, I've heard many single women say they refuse to make major purchases until they're married. They are led to believe that their life isn't complete because they're not married. Woman of God, God wants to bless you with the desires of your heart before you get married!! God doesn't want you to place Him in constraints, He wants to show you that He can take care of you better than anyone could ever imagine!!! If you're waiting to be married to live your best life- it could take several years before your spouse comes, then what?? What kind of regret would you have? What if you never get married?? What about your offspring who's depending on you to lay a foundation for them? Whatever you do, do it with your legacy in mind. Building a legacy for your children and your children's children is all part of God's plan, married or not, male or female. What plans are you making so that your children don't suffer the way you have? What are you building now that would impact your offspring? You may not have a lot of money, but you can impart financial wisdom into them. Teach them what you had to learn the hard way so that they don't make the same mistakes you've made.

Most of us learned the hard way about credit, debt and saving money, we learned by trial and error. And some of us never heard of investing our money until we got older.

Teach your children what the word of God says about finances. What God says about sowing seeds and paying tithes. Teach your children how to apply the word of God concerning their finances which is the best advice you could give them. It doesn't matter how much you teach them about building financially, if they're not taught God's way, they will only spin their wheels!! I taught my son about tithing and sowing when he was very young so that he doesn't suffer like I did. I suffered because of what I didn't know. Teach your children what the word of God says about blessings and curses as well as be an example to them. And when God blesses you let them know it's because of your obedience from tithing and giving the reason that you're blessed. As you are an example to your children it will make a great impact on your children and the generations to come.

A Spiritual Inheritance- Despite the fact that you are single, it's God's desire for you to leave a spiritual legacy for your children that will be passed down through out your generations until Jesus returns. When most people think of legacy, they think of someone dying but it is not about death. It's about living a good life, living for those you love and being a good example for your generations to come. What type of legacy are you building? Building a legacy is much more than providing a financial inheritance for your children. There are other ways to leave an inheritance such as being a good mother, wife, daughter, sister, or friend. The words you speak, the advice and the wisdom that you give will have a major impact on others even when you're long gone. The people you are surrounded by will never forget how you have impacted their lives especially your children.

Teaching your children about God and taking them to church are a few examples of building a spiritual legacy. What better way to build a legacy?? You may not have money to build a legacy financially, but everyone can build a spiritual legacy.

My grandmother was a single woman, she didn't have any money to leave her children or grandchildren, but she left a huge impact. She built a spiritual legacy which has affected her children and grandchildren who have affected their children and so on. She took us to church, instilled the word of God in us and taught us how to pray.

Not only did she inspire us, but she inspired others as well. Her legacy lives on and will never be forgotten. She had a responsibility and that was to teach her descendants about God, and she didn't hold back. She was more concerned with leaving a rich spiritual inheritance than a financial inheritance. And to this day, her children, grand-children, and even her great-children love and serve God. No, we're not perfect but we know who God is. But what if my grandmother would have listened to the enemy's voice, that she's worthless because she was single? That she needs to go out and enjoy her life and find her a man like all the other single women? The enemy would have destroyed her, her offspring and descendants!! Why? Because her focus would have been on seeking after worldly things than what matters most, and that was to teach her children, grand-children, and her family about Jesus Christ!!

The word of God says- *Deuteronomy 30:19-* says- *I call heaven and earth to record this day against you, that I have set before you life and death, blessings and cursing: therefore choose life, that both thou and thy seed may live."*

You can cause your family to reign in blessings or reign in curses. Our job is to influence our children to live a Godly life. Building a spiritual legacy and living a Godly life before your children will cause you to have a direct impact on them. When we were young, we couldn't understand why my grandmother spent most of her time worshipping, praying and reading the Bible. My brothers and I would make fun of her because we didn't understand. At times she would laugh at us for making fun of her, but she knew that she was leaving a mark on us to serve God and to love Him. She wasn't worried about being single, our salvation was her number one priority. She pointed us in the direction of our Lord!!!

Psalms 127:4 -NIV-says- "Like arrows in the hand of a warrior are the children of one's youth."

We as parents have the ability to guide our children in the right or the wrong direction.

SINGLE, SATISFIED & SET APART

If you are a single mother, you have a great assignment and living a Godly life before your children is one of them. Teach your children about God, teach them how to pray, and bring them to church. Teach them to tithe and sow. You're building a legacy not a tradition. Teach them to acknowledge God in everything and to seek first the kingdom of God and God will bless them. Teach them that they're blessed because of God. In the Bible after the death of Joshua, there arose another generation who didn't know God. And because they weren't taught, they had no reverence or fear for God. No one carried on the assignment to teach the next generation. Our job is to teach our children and to raise them in the fear and the reverence of God!!

Ephesians 6:4 says, "And ye fathers, provoke not your children to wrath but bring them up in the nurture and admonition of the Lord."

Proverbs 22:6- says – "train up a child in the way he should go: and when he is old, he will not depart from it."

Single mothers, don't get so caught up in wanting a husband so bad that you fail to teach your children about God. You have a generation that is dependent on you and you owe it to them to do the right thing!! Don't allow your legacy to die because you are single. You birthed kings, queens, spiritual giants, and world-changers who need you to lead and guide them and prepare them for their future. You may be single, but you have everything it takes to build a powerful spiritual legacy for your children and your future generations.

ABOUT THE AUTHOR

Vinokia Johnson was born and raised in Shreveport, Louisiana where she lived for thirty years. Being obedient to the voice of God she moved to Houston, Tx where she now resides. She is the proud mother of one son Marcellas Baker, who is twenty-three years old. She is a Registered Nurse (RN) and has been a nurse for twenty-two years. She specializes in patients with Special Needs and Pediatric Health. Due to her many trials and adversities, she began to pursue God concerning the will of God for her life. She discovered that her purpose is to help lead the way for other women with similar situations that she's overcome. Her trust in God has caused her to withstand many obstacles placed before her.

Because of her struggles as a single mother, she has a special place in her heart for single women and children. Driven by her passion to help women, she finds joy in sharing her powerful testimony. She acknowledges that her strong belief in God came from her grandmother, the late Malinda Washington. Pressing against all oppositions and against all odds, she's determined to fulfill her God's given purpose.

STAY CONNECTED

  amazon.com

   BARNES&NOBLE

@VINOKIAJOHNSON
WWW.VINOKIAJOHNSON.COM

Made in the USA
Middletown, DE
02 March 2022

61962901R00066